Is praise *always* a **good** thing?

Reflecting on praise, encouragement and appreciation

Ian Smith

Acknowledgements

The publishers would like to thank the following for permission to reproduce copyright material on the pages listed: HarperCollins for the extract on page 3 from *In Search of Excellence* by Tom Peters and Robert Waterman; Prentice Hall for the extracts on pages 6, 7 and 8 from *Teaching Through Encouragement* by Robert Martin.

The extract on page 3 from *Recent Research in Mathematics Education 5 16* is Crown copyright and is reproduced with the permission of the Controller of Her Majesty's Stationery Office.

First published 1998

Reprinted by Learning and Teaching Scotland 2007

© Scottish Consultative Council on the Curriculum 1998

ISBN 978 185955 155 4

Introduction

This paper is one of a series published by Scottish CCC as a follow up to the discussion paper *Teaching for Effective Learning* published in 1996. The papers pick up on topics that have proved to be of particular interest or concern to teachers.

Designed to stimulate both thinking and action, the papers provide an overview of a particular aspect of learning and teaching by highlighting the latest research and good practice. Readers are encouraged to relate current understandings about the topic to their own beliefs and practice.

This paper examines the issues concerned with praise, encouragement and appreciation and suggests some practical ways in which teachers might use these more effectively.

The views expressed in the paper are those of the author and do not necessarily reflect the views of Scottish CCC.

Accentuate the positive

This seems to be a common piece of advice being offered to teachers these days. One example of this is the recommendation in *Standards and Quality in Scottish Schools 1992 95* (SOEID, 1996) that teachers, particularly in secondary schools, ought to 'make more frequent and effective use of praise'.

The vast majority of teachers would accept this recommendation. They agree that it is right to highlight praise as an issue. Used effectively, praise can help build self esteem, help people to master basic skills and work harder for certain extrinsic goals.

However, simply exhorting teachers to use praise more frequently and more effectively will not help them to do so – however willing they are. Praise is a complex issue.

Most of us are not as positive as we think we are

One thing is certain: most of us are not as positive as we think we are. Recent research in England using a sample of 130 secondary teachers showed that 90 per cent believed that they were more positive than negative. When these teachers were observed over a number of weeks, it was discovered that they made three times as many positive remarks as negative ones when focusing on academic work. When focusing on classroom behaviour, they made three times as many negative remarks as positive ones. Positive remarks for academic work decreased the older the pupils became. Another survey of 50 London junior schools by Peter Mortimore found that teachers spent less than one per cent of their time giving praise.

Let's not be too hard on ourselves here, however. Put down remarks are a generally accepted form of communication in our society, in families and between young people, although often they are meant 'jokingly' or as a way of conveying affection. Recent research in the UK based on observations of children both at home and in school showed that on an average day they received 460 negative or critical comments compared to 75 positive or supportive comments. This mirrors research in the US which showed that in the average home negative comments outnumber positive comments by five to one.

- **Do you think you make more positive than negative comments to pupils?**
- **Would this be true for classroom behaviour as well as academic work?**

Is praise always a good thing?

There is plenty of advice around on how to use praise effectively. The following criteria offered by OFSTED are fairly typical of what is considered to be good practice.

> *'Praise should be contingent – it must depend on some particular thing the pupil has done rather than on their general performance. Some would say it should be for a specific behaviour not for the child.*
>
> *It should be specific – it should identify the specific behaviour being praised and the reason why so that the pupil knows what aspect of their work is being singled out for praise.*
>
> *The praise must be credible; praise that follows a 'formula' (i.e. is always expressed in the same way) or which sounds insincere is likely to be ineffective since pupils can see through this very quickly. Praise should be spontaneous and expressed in a variety of ways.'*
>
> Mike Askew and Dylan William, *Recent Research in Mathematics Education 5–16*, 1995

A good example of giving praise in a spontaneous, immediate and original manner comes from *In Search of Excellence* by Tom Peters and Robert Waterman.

> *'At Foxboro, a technical advance was desperately needed for survival in the company's early days. Late one evening, a scientist rushed into the president's office with a working prototype. Dumbfounded at the excellence of the solution and bemused about how to reward it, the president bent forward in his chair, rummaged through most of the drawers in his desk, found something, leaned over the desk to the scientist, and said, 'Here!' In his hand was a banana, the only reward he could immediately put his hands on. From that point on, the small 'gold banana' pin has been the highest accolade for scientific achievement at Foxboro.'*
>
> Tom Peters and Robert Waterman, *In Search of Excellence*, 1984

Books on classroom discipline, which focus on pupil behaviour and what teachers can do to control it, tend to stress praise very strongly.

> *'What's the best way you can motivate students? Praise. The most effective? Praise. What positive recognition can you give to your students at any time? Under all circumstances? Praise.'*
>
> Lee Canter and Marlene Canter, *Assertive Discipline*, 1992

But is praise always a good thing? As the OFSTED report quoted above points out, there is no simple relationship between the use of praise and pupil achievement.

For instance, giving praise where it is not due is counterproductive. Everyone knows in themselves when they have or have not achieved something meaningful. If a student does not deserve praise that student will know. They may initially accept the teacher's praise but it won't last long. Fairly soon the student will see that they have accomplished nothing, and the teacher's credibility will have been damaged.

It can also be counterproductive to praise learners for succeeding in a task which is not very difficult. Learners may take this to mean that they are not very smart. Margaret Donaldson suggests this applies to very young children.

> *'When it comes to self esteem, not even a very young child depends entirely for his judgements on the views of others. For he can often see for himself how he is doing. Thus a very important part of the job of a teacher is to guide the child towards tasks where he will be able objectively to do well, but not too easily, not without difficulties to be mastered.'*
>
> Margaret Donaldson, *Children's Minds*, 1986

Praise, therefore, is a complex issue. It is difficult to examine in isolation, as it is bound up with many other issues such as self esteem, self belief, fear of failure, learning styles, control, responsibility and culture. Like most things in teaching there are no easy answers which will work for everyone everywhere.

Can praise actually be harmful?

There are many who believe that praise, even when used appropriately and according to the criteria above, can be oversold as a technique to increase motivation and control behaviour, and that it can have harmful side effects. They stress the importance of more subtle and genuine approval (what Carl Rogers refers to as 'transparent realness'); the importance of building positive relationships through encouragement and appreciation; and the need to help learners to develop their own views of themselves, of each other and of the world.

Alfie Kohn is the most outspoken critic of praise. In his book *Punished by Rewards* he talks about the 'praise problem' and calls praise 'a bribe'. He argues that the most important question to ask about praise is 'what is its purpose?' and he believes it is often used to control. He suggests that what we need to do is not to stop using praise but to think about the nature of the praise we use, what we say and how. In particular, we need to examine why we are praising.

> 'With every comment we make, and specifically every compliment we give, we need to ask whether we are helping that individual to feel a sense of control over their life. Are we encouraging him to make his own judgements about what constitutes a good performance or a desirable action? Are we contributing to or at least preserving his ability to choose what kind of person to be? Or are we attempting to manipulate his behaviour? First then we need to examine our own motives.'
>
> Alfie Kohn, *Punished by Rewards*, 1993

Viewed in this light, praise and rewards begin to appear counterproductive. They can be seen as a means of inducing people to conform, of manipulating and controlling people, and even as a form of bribery. Often praise conveys the message: 'You can have my approval only by doing what I decide is right for you'. This is what Alistair Smith calls 'positive conditional' ('I am glad to see you are on time again' or 'This is your best piece of work so far').

Overuse of praise, it is argued, can actually limit the opportunity for students to develop their own decision making ability and can reduce their ability to self evaluate. In effect, it can disempower people. Self confident people need less praise. They feel good about themselves and are better able to appreciate themselves without being dependent on the approval of others. The challenge for teachers is to help pupils build their self confidence.

People react differently to different kinds of praise

Some people seem to have less need for praise than others, either because they are better able to evaluate the quality of their work for themselves or because they have a stronger self image. To others, praise is extremely important because without positive feedback they will assume that they have not done well.

Different personalities also prefer different kinds of praise. Some people want, indeed need, appreciation for who they are. You cannot tell such people too often that you enjoy their company or you appreciate their work. Others prefer feedback about their competence. For them praise must be specific and credible. For them statements like 'well done!' have little meaning unless you explain why.

- How important is praise, encouragement and appreciation to you?

- How do you react to different kinds of praise, encouragement and appreciation?

Use praise, but use it carefully

So what is to be done? Kohn describes working with teachers who felt unable to stop praising their students since many of them came from desperate circumstances, from loveless homes, and were therefore in great need of the teacher's support and approval. Kohn agrees, but suggests that such students need approval without strings attached; that what they require is unconditional love, not praise which is conditional.

Here are some suggestions which may help you to consider how to use praise, encouragement and appreciation. The first and most important is to use praise, but use it carefully. A lot depends on your own personality and style, the relationship you have already established with your students and the culture within which you work in the school.

Whom you praise, encourage or show your appreciation to, and when and how you do it, is very much a matter for personal and professional judgement. Most of the time these judgements are made on the spur of the moment and without thinking, and are based on your ways of working, your beliefs and values as a person and as a teacher. It pays to be more aware of what these are and how they affect the way you praise, encourage and show your appreciation.

Robert Martin has some specific suggestions about how to use praise carefully.

> **Avoid using praise to soften criticism.** *This is a common tactic; when someone says 'You did a good job' and then pauses, we anticipate "but ..." followed by criticism.*
>
> **Avoid using praise to pressure students.** *'You always do so well!' often becomes transformed into pressure to do well all the time. Because of such pressure some people feel discouraged by praise because they are afraid they won't be able to repeat their success.*
>
> **Be careful, praise may be resented.** *Praise can be condescending, maintaining the superiority of one person over another, in which case it will be resented. Students may also resent praise when it isolates them from their peers by singling them out or by embarrassing them.*
>
> **Be slow to praise.** *A positive evaluation is still an evaluation, and many people are uncomfortable with or even suspicious of evaluations, whether positive or negative.*
>
> **When you do praise, praise those who need it.** *Praise is most likely to go to those pupils who need it least. Praising only those students who have achieved a certain superiority is likely to encourage students to feel superior and other students to feel inferior.*
>
> **Don't push positive thinking.** *When a pupil feels upset or discouraged, don't try to humour them with positive thinking ('You can do it' and similar expressions). Respecting pupils' feelings will be more positive in the long run.*
>
> Robert Martin, *Teaching Through Encouragement*, 1980

Dare to show your appreciation a bit more

At first glance, 'appreciation' may appear to be just another term for 'praise', but there are important differences. Praise ('You are doing a good job', 'You are a good student') is an evaluation. Appreciation ('I appreciate the work you are doing', 'I like having you in my class') is an expression of feeling rather than an evaluation. Instead of conveying the message 'you are good', it conveys the message 'I like you, I like what you are doing, I like the way you are behaving'. It demonstrates positive regard and it involves taking a risk, sharing something of yourself.

Appreciation, then, is about sharing personal feelings with another person. Saying things like:

- I appreciate your friendship.
- I enjoy the way you read.
- I appreciate your cheerfulness.
- I appreciate the way you keep plugging away.
- I enjoy the way you use colour so freely in your pictures.

- **Do you show your appreciation of your pupils and, if so, how?**

- **What reservations do you have about showing appreciation?**

Think about using encouragement rather than praise

Robert Martin describes encouragement as the process of imparting courage and confidence. He favours encouragement rather than praise.

Look for and focus on strengths. *Attempting to change people by focusing on their weaknesses rarely works. It reinforces feelings of discouragement and helplessness. Even someone who is talented and successful can be devastated by destructively focusing on weakness. It is possible to find strengths in all students and even more crucial that you find them and recognise them in those who are having difficulty.*

Take pupils seriously. *The basis for encouraging people is taking them seriously. There is no substitute for sincere interest. Without a willingness to become involved with pupils as human beings, the practices suggested in books and articles on effective teaching are meaningless.*

Take an interest. *Take time to listen and observe. Be careful about giving help until it is wanted. When you are taking others seriously you are trying to learn as well as teach, to find out what pupils think and what their attitudes are.*

Build on student interest. *Be prepared to change a lesson to build on the interests and strengths of the pupils. Often this can be done without changing the essence of what you are trying to do.*

Ask for help. *Involve pupils in tasks and decisions so that they feel they have a contribution to make. Few things are more encouraging than being part of a group where your contribution is needed and appreciated.*

Put success within reach. *This is different from manufacturing success. Easy success, excessive praise and overemphasis on being successful can create more problems than they solve. Yet the experience of success no matter how small, or of completing a task no matter how simple, is essential to encouragement.*

Look for mistakes that make sense. *Mistakes are often the result of a logical though incorrect approach to solving a problem. Teachers who do not realise when a mistake makes sense are likely to discourage pupils from thinking. Listen. Ask yourself why a pupil has answered the way she has and show you understand.*

Robert Martin, *Teaching Through Encouragement*, 1980

A well known Americanism, 'positive strokes', is relevant in any discussion of appreciation and encouragement.

'A stroke can be defined as a unit of attention. Humans need them for survival and growth. Without strokes, positive or negative, we wither. Strokes can be given or received, be accepted or discounted, be positive or negative, conditional or unconditional, plastic or real. A positive stroke is a unit of attention which makes the receiver feel good about him or herself.'

Alistair Smith, *Accelerated Learning in the Classroom*, 1996

'Encouragement', 'appreciation' or 'strokes', all these approaches share one significant difference from praise: they do not include judgement or evaluation.

Some ideas to consider

- Use a tally counter to monitor how often you use praise, encouragement or show your appreciation of pupils in a lesson.
- Use the points about kinds of praise to discuss with colleagues what you prefer and what you use.

- Work with a colleague whom you know and trust to devise a checklist using some of the questions in this article to observe each other working. Agree to identify one or two areas you will work on.
- Challenge pupils themselves to prohibit put down remarks (for example, by establishing a 'no put down zone').
- Use affirming messages on the walls and in displays around the classroom.
- Encourage pupils to develop a positive vocabulary; to develop the habit of exchanging statements of appreciation.

Key points

- Most of us, either as teachers, parents or managers, tend to be less positive than we think we are.
- There is no doubt that it pays for teachers to be positive.
- Teachers are being exhorted to use praise more.
- There is a lot of advice about how to praise appropriately.
- Many argue that praise is not always the best way to be positive.
- There are different kinds of praise, conditional and unconditional.
- Conditional praise is often used to control behaviour.
- Some argue that too much conditional praise can actually be harmful, that it can disempower and actually undermine confidence.
- People react differently to different kinds of praise.
- It is important to be aware of the purpose of positive comments.
- Focusing on appreciation, on encouragement rather than praise, can be more effective in building motivation, confidence and a sense of responsibility.

References

Askew, Mike and William, Dylan, *Recent Research in Mathematics Education 5–16, An OFSTED Review of Research*, London: HMSO, 1995, ISBN 0 11 350049 1

Canter, Lee and Canter, Marlene, *Assertive Discipline: Positive Behaviour Management for Today's Classroom*, Santa Monica: Lee Canter and Associates, 1992, ISBN 0 939007 45 2

Curwin, Richard and Mendlar, Allan, *Discipline with Dignity*, Virginia, USA: ASCD, 1998

Donaldson, Margaret, *Children's Minds*, London: Fontana Collins, 1986, ISBN 0 00 686122 9

Gibbs, Jeanne, *Tribes: A New Way of Learning and Being Together*, California, USA: Center Source Systems, 1995

Jenson, Eric, *Super Teaching*, USA: Turning Point, 1995, ISBN 0 96378 320 3

* Kohn, Alfie, *Beyond Discipline: From Compliance to Community*, Virginia, USA: ASCD, 1996, ISBN 0 87120 270 0

Kohn, Alfie, *Punished by Rewards*, New York: Houghton Mifflin, 1993

* Martin, Robert, *Teaching Through Encouragement*, Hemel Hempstead, Herts: Prentice Hall, 1980, ISBN 0 13896 266 9

Peters, Tom and Waterman, Robert, *In Search of Excellence: Lessons from America's Best run Companies*, New York: Harper and Row, 1984, ISBN 0 06 338002 1

Scottish CCC, *The Heart of the Matter*, Dundee: Scottish CCC, 1995, ISBN 1 85955 088 6

Smith, Alistair, *Accelerated Learning in the Classroom*, Stafford: Network Educational Press, 1996, ISBN 1 85539 034 5

HM Inspectors of Schools Audit Unit, *Standards and Quality in Scottish Schools 1992–95*, Edinburgh: The Scottish Office Education and Industry Department, 1996, ISBN 0 7480 3136 7

Wheldall, Kevin and Merrett, Frank, *Positive Teaching in the Secondary School*, London: Paul Chapman, 1989

Those texts highlighted with an asterisk are particularly recommended.